LIGHTHOUSE

Navigate the emotional storms of life and discover the power within you

MICHAEL JAMES

LIGHTHOUSE - Navigate the emotional stor⌐
life and discover the power within you

Copyright © 2016 Michael James
www.michaeljames.be

Published by EMERGING JOURNEYS
www.emergingjourneys.com

Cover design and conception: Michael James/Louise Chu

A catalogue record for this book is available from the British Library

ISBN: 978-0-9929997-1-1

CONTENTS

FOREWORD

It is a great honour for me to be invited to write the foreword for this groundbreaking book. In my view Michael James will go down as one of the most revolutionary leaders in the consciousness movement this century. His wisdom is already in a league with the greats such as Louise Hay, Esther Hicks and Wayne Dyer. However, that said, in these fast and furious times we are now living in Michael's methods for soothing the soul when in times of turmoil and torment are in my view unsurpassed.

Everybody encounters storms of the mind and emotion whether they admit it or not. For centuries, especially in the UK, there has been generations of conditioning where you bite your lip and just "get on with it" and if anyone asks you "How are you really?" you are expected to say "I'm fine" or run for your life! This is where Michael (who I affectionately refer to at times as *Archangel Michael*) comes in. In that precise moment when we want to run because we cannot face or deal with what we are feeling, this is the moment to pick up *Lighthouse*. On every page there is a tonic to soothe your emotional crossing so that you may reach safely to shore. What I love about Michael is that he is the "real deal". The methods that he has brought through in this book have been mined through facing his own suffering, like the deep sea divers that have to swim down to the depths of the ocean to bring up the pearls and corals to the surface. Hence the value of his wisdom is priceless.

In my case, I have had the incredible good fortune of knowing Michael as a dear friend for 13 years and so for me it has been like having an audio version of this book at the end of the phone through all my challenges. Whenever I have felt that my boat is about to be smashed against the rocks, whether it be about my career or personal life, Michael's soothing voice at the end of the phone has been my absolute anchor; a "lighthouse" that I can eternally trust will be there.

The wisdom that pours through him, that has felt at times as though is comes from an angelic realm of guidance, uplifts me instantly. By the end of my dialogue with Michael I no longer feel I need to obliterate my circumstances, for example a dismissive boss, an argument with a loved one, a neglectful colleague, financial concerns etc... To the contrary he inspires me to see another view and guides me to embrace my circumstances as a "workout" for my soul to evolve, and he helps me to see the hidden gift or promise in every situation. Michael has frequently said to me "All is well" and you feel that when he speaks those simple words that they are actually true. I am then able to move forward with courage - even though the storms may well still be brewing however my mast is now set in a new and empowering direction that steers me out of danger!

If Michael could speak directly on the phone to each individual on the planet who is in trouble, I am sure he would if he could! For this reason, for all souls who are making this perilous crossing called "Life", Michael James offers you *Lighthouse*. Keep this book close to your person each day as like a lighthouse it will never fail you. Thank you Michael James.

With great love and respect,

Nikki Slade, Kirtan leader and pioneer in voice and sound work

INTRODUCTION

We all have different ideas about what makes for a good life, and what is the meaning of life, but one thing is true for everyone: We all want to feel good; we all want to feel *confident* - about ourselves and about life. When we feel this way - relaxed, clear-minded, excited, enthusiastic and sure of ourselves - our life works. We have the best ideas, and our impulses are right-on. We are in the right place at the right time. We know our reason for being and our life's purpose. We feel attractive and we like ourselves. We feel whole, complete and fulfilled, and we experience the best life has to offer wherever we go.

However, there are times when you don't feel this way: fearful, insecure, anxious, resentful, lonely, irritated or depressed, for instance, and this book gives you ways for dealing with those emotional storms when you are in the middle of it; to help you get back on track and enjoying life again. This book is based on real-life research I've gathered from working with people and developing ideas on how to deal with life no matter what's going on. It is short, simple and effective.

Throughout our lives we have been taught that the best approach is to think things through when they go wrong and to endlessly analyse our problems; to try to figure out how best to live life. But this rarely works; instead keeping us stuck in our problems and solving little. This book is about the opposite of fixing: It's about stepping back; it's about relaxation and the practices offered within it are proven ways to relax and calm the mind. Relaxing doesn't mean being passive. When our bodies and minds are relaxed we reach our optimum capacity. We get "in our zone". We are then able to deal with life in the best possible way, by discovering new ideas and knowing exactly which action to take at the right time.

Through my work and life experiences, I've discovered that some of the most incredible people feel the lowest before they "get it". Regardless of how you may feel in any one moment, you are the *opposite* of a wreck. You are the sanest of the sane, in fact. It seems that the kind of pain that comes with overthinking things somehow wakes you up to realising that *you are not the mind.* You only seem to understand this when the mind causes you some kind of hell. So it's actually a gift when you feel off centre, as you will discover for yourself in this book.

Just like a lighthouse serves as a beacon to guide ships into safety and ultimately freedom, this book will guide you back to your own calm and confidence so that you don't *need* the lighthouse, because you are one. You don't *need* anything "out there" to make you feel enough - because you are already enough. And from this standpoint you can begin to enjoy life.

The part of this book which will be used the most is the Quick Reference Section. If you want instant soothing, turn to the level that best describes your current mood: *Feeling Low, Feeling Uninspired* or *Feeling Good,* open at random and begin reading.

A NEW WAY OF LOOKING AT LIFE

Challenges are a part of life: They're how we evolve

Everyone experiences challenges in their lives, even though it may seem that many people don't, as they deal with their problems in private and try to "look good" for the world. I've never met anyone who is 100% happy all the time, and there is nothing wrong with that. It is part of life to experience tension and feel less than our best sometimes. Tension and not feeling good are more than okay, in fact, because it is the tension and challenges which create the best opportunities to move forward in life. Often our greatest insights, ideas and experiences arise after a period of challenge.

An example of the advantages of tension is a workout session at the gym. As you exercise, you deliberately create physical tension to build muscle. The greater the tension, the more the muscle builds. You don't fight the tension or condemn it. In much the same way, life's challenges and resistances help you evolve to become the best you can be. The greater the tension, the greater potential there is for positive transformation.

We've heard people say how their most difficult relationships prepared them for their ideal love relationship. Some of the richest people came from poverty: we hear of their rags-to-riches stories where the past challenges of a poor life paved the way for a wealthy life. And some of the most life-loving, happy, optimistic people were once the most depressed. It's the same with life in general: *all* parts of life can be regarded as positive, both the good times and the bad - the challenges evolve us and the times we feel good are the "post gym rest" where we relax and receive these new benefits.

The above ideas help explain why so often when success is coming, the opposite counterpart - thoughts and experiences of failure - can come into your mind, as they are both key, connected players in the evolution of life. So it makes sense that if you have big dreams you may have also experienced big insecurities and self-criticism; they're both exciting signs of your coming evolution.

In this book you will find proven ways to make peace with all parts of life no matter what's going on. In this way, you will experience the benefits arising from any tension and stress.

States of Mind

Many people think that they are their mind and they are their thoughts - but they are not. Who we really are doesn't think in this "mind chatter" way at all; but communicates with impulse, intuition and knowing, as you'll discover in this book.

Remember a time when you felt "in the zone" - having one of those peak experiences of life? We've all had those moments where life was just perfect in the moment. You weren't thinking, you were *being*. That's what this book is about - a practical way to get tuned into You: that space where you feel whole, complete and fulfilled, right now. Think of fine tuning a radio until you get a clear signal, or a Formula One car getting a "tune up" in the pit lane, mid race. It's about being tuned up and tuned in to who you are - tuned into your centre; tuned to your light; into what you could call your Real Self. When you are attuned to your Real Self, you feel good. You feel confident. You know what to do. You love your life. *Life works.*

When we were very young children, we didn't judge and analyse. Everything and everyone was "just as it is" - with no opinion attached. We didn't think, we were just being ourselves, and we allowed the world and everyone in it to be as they were, too. This approach didn't make us weak - it made us powerful. We had a strong gut feeling about who felt safe and who didn't, but we didn't attack or reason with our thoughts the way our "adult" mind does. We didn't think - we *appreciated* life. *We were our Real Selves.*

In short- in our natural state we are very powerful. *Time to get back to that.*

Your journey back to You

There's something powerful in turning away from our connection and then later rediscovering it. There is huge learning in coming back home after a time away, rather than simply staying at home. Many great epic tales have someone wandering off the path - a fairly ordinary person - and then coming back a hero. When we go on a journey, we learn new things, and bring them back to empower and transform our usual lives.

And so this journey back into our Real Self is just the same - with not a second wasted on the idea that we've somehow gone off track - but instead the realisation that it was all part of the plan.

Time to return to who we really are and receive the rewards of our life's journey that we may have believed to be "off track", but was actually very much "on track".

Being our Real Self: The evolution of Life

In the theory of evolution, as a species encounters a challenge it creates the potential for expansion. So in the bigger picture, both the relaxed times and the challenges are all part of the process. The slings and arrows the species faces are an essential part of life. Species which don't encounter challenges don't evolve and become extinct. The Dodo is a famous example, which had very few predators and an abundance of food nearby. For a long time, it was in its comfort zone. When challenges finally arrived in the form of imported predators, it was done for.

We think we encounter challenges in real physical form - but our challenges are mostly in the form of encountering thoughts in our mind rather than the experiences we have. *It's the thoughts we have about what's going on that provides our pain (and corresponding evolution) rather than what actually happened. This thinking indicates that we have stepped aside from who we really are - and also indicates our evolution.*

So when we go into thoughts and feel that corresponding uncomfortable feeling - expansion happens. If we continue to dwell in thoughts, we don't tune into this expanded us. The results of the evolution happen on what you could call the Real

Self transmission; it's like the ultimate multimedia broadcast playing the best of who you are. It *is* who you are. Imagine watching a television channel: something unpleasant happens on the program you are watching, and at the same time something equally good happens, too - *but on another channel, playing simultaneously.*

You often don't see the effects of this evolution, because you are lost in overthinking - and the painful feeling you feel is telling you that you are lost. This painful feeling is actually a call to come back to centre. It's like a smoke alarm going off and rather than putting out the fire, you don't get the message, but instead just sit and complain and suffer over the noise rather than do anything. *The alarm in this case is a nudge to "change channel" - to move out of thinking and sync up with the Real You perspective.*

Most of us know the pain of not shifting when this emotional smoke alarm goes off. At these times if can seem like the mind is in control of us, rather than a device we can enter into and out of at will. We keep on thinking, driving deeper into our intellect and into more and more complexity - when a more successful approach would be to *step back* from our mind and its mind chatter. Yet this is just a bad habit - and bad habits can be replaced with beneficial habits.

Certain people seem to have stronger emotions. When you don't know how to work with your mind, having strong emotions becomes a personal hell - as it did with me*. But when you understand how to work with your mind, strong emotions can become a great guide. When we understand that the emotional pain means we are *evolving*, which is good, and we are going into thinking - then emotions become a reminder to "course correct" and centre ourselves, which is where our best life is.

You can read about my experiences in "My Story" at the end of this book

The Real Self

The Real Self has been called different names throughout history: the soul, the true self, the divine spark, the higher self, the inner light, the eternal self... It doesn't matter what you call it - but everyone knows when they are synced up with it: You feel self-empowered, you feel connected, you feel free-flowing and happy, with a natural confidence. You *are* confidence. It's your inner god or goddess; it's your aerial view perspective that simply knows what to do at all times, feels great, looks great and shines with a relaxed self-assurance. It's the you that was your natural state before you learnt the disconnected ways of the world and covered your light with thought patterns. This state of being never went away and glows ever brighter. When you disconnect from who you are, it becomes brighter still. It shines steadfastly like a lighthouse, covered over but waiting to be revealed in every moment. It has that "in the zone" feeling where you don't think, you are simply "being". When you are unattached to thought and fully in your Real Self, you are naturally magnetic and charismatic. People are drawn to you.

Although the Real Self is a thoughtless state, it is not an empty place. As you drop out of the mind chatter, the door is open to your Real "thought"; which is less like thought and more like a computer download which comes in the form of impulses, instincts, intuition and knowing: projected ideas and insights rather than reasoning or analysis. If you are in "mind chatter" - you are not in your Real Self, you have "static in the radio" and you cannot see life clearly.

Master musicians don't think up a song - they feel the music, and write it down. Authors explain how they "received" their bestselling novel - they didn't think it up, they let it in. Athletes get into "no thought" and "channel" their world class performance; inventors "download" their ideas when in a state of no thought. There is nothing wrong with thought - it is the thinking workout which created the ideas to begin with - but without the ability to let loose of thought - the ideas wouldn't be received and made manifest.

True intelligence comes from the Real Self; in the gaps between thoughts. There is nothing wrong with thinking - but everything you want is revealed when you are out of your overthinking rather than in it - *and so you want to make finding a way to drop out of your overthinking mind and drop into your Real Self a priority.*

Tuning into the Real You

Your Real Self mind occurs just beyond your mind chatter mind. It's a constant transmission; a resonance forever being broadcast and forever evolving as a result of, quite often, those experiences you find difficult. Your work is not about deliberately thinking thoughts, like with "positive thinking". It's about dropping out of the lower level "static" thinking mind altogether. Practically, this is like manually tuning a radio. As you turn the dial you can hear the static lessening and the broadcast getting more vivid and clear. You don't *think* the words on the broadcast yourself, you *listen* for them. Just as you don't need to tamper with the individual programs on your television and make them into something else - you change channels to the program you want to watch - it's the same with our life: our job isn't to fix ourselves, but to tune into our already-created perfection. *Our job is to tune into the light of our Real Self and then watch as the world mirrors it back.*

Thoughts, the language of the lower self mind, will tell you a million and one things, on and on they go, speaking nonsense. In the contemporary world, we are taught that this is called "intelligence" - the ability to think a lot. But indulging in mind chatter is the opposite of intelligence. It is the barrier to true intelligence, in fact. Our job is to tune into our Real Self; that place of no thought - but it's not about "trying not to think". When we try to not do something, we often do it more: *what we resist, persists.*

In truth, it's always a "good day", behind the clouds of thought

The sun always shines behind the clouds. In fact, it's always a sunny day, if you go high enough above the cloud cover. In the same way, clouds of thoughts may cover the Real Self, but it's always there steadfastly shining.

Tune into the Real Self - *and then follow it's guidance.*

Once we do what we can to tune into our Real Self (we'll come to how to do that in the Quick Reference Section), we want to follow the inner guidance that comes in the form of those inner nudges and insights that feel very different to mind chatter.

"Go left", you might feel - and be guided to enter a shop when something you want is on sale. "Help that person" may be the nudge you get when you see someone struggling with a shopping bag. "Go to that event tonight", it may say. People want the intuitive voice of their Real Self to keep them in a comfort zone. But it's not like that. At first, it might be a challenge to follow these "gut feelings". The lower self (or "lower level") mind chatter may offer all kinds of excuses not to follow this instruction - much of it's reasoning revolving around "what will they think of me?" (which is one of the lower self mind's favourite things to say). I remember someone telling me that "People will judge you anyway - whether you are being yourself or a people pleaser - so why not just *be yourself?*" Great advice that was.

With practice you learn not to question the Real Self's impulses whilst ignoring the lower self mind's fear-based chatter, and you follow what this guidance says, as it always leads you to the right place at the right time. The right actions to take will be guided by your Real Self and you will know what to do.

Real Self summary

- The Real Self is instinctual, it's that "heart mind" or "solar plexus gut feeling" as opposed to the analytical "head mind" of the false self mindset. The Real Self is the You experienced when you are clear-minded. The false self occurs in the realm of overthinking.
- Thinking is the language of the "ego" - which is another word for our lower or false self mind. Intuition is the language of the Real Self - which comes to you in the form of impressions, impulses or instincts. When you don't feel good - it means you are in your false self perception and you have gone into the level of overthinking - and it's a nudge to be You again instead.
- Pain is when we go into overthinking. Feeling good is when we drop out of thoughts. Both are ok. Battling the current of life is good, it evolves us - but it is in the relaxation into the Real Self where we receive the "gains" from our battles and our overthinking.
- It's not about "positive thinking" - it's about dropping out of thoughts altogether.
- The primary problem we can have is that we are in thinking (the false self). And the solution is to get into the Real Self. You are either in thoughts - or you are synced with your Real Self. It's one or the other.
- Waves of thoughts will come - that's life - and that's how we evolve. Leave them to do their

work of evolving you - and step aside. Rise above them with the practical ideas in this book.

- If occasionally a wave of thought and emotion takes you under - remember it's just a "workout"; it's evolution. What Olympic champion doesn't go under sometimes? You want to welcome-in tension, as it is this which expands and evolves you.
- The Real Self part of you is evolving with every challenge or difficulty you face. Every time you think, your Real Self evolves. No matter what you do, the Real Self always gets more powerful and more confident.
- Fearlessly follow the guidance of your Real Self - it's always accurate.

Syncing up with your Real Self

We can't think our way out of a problem though many of us keep on trying to. There are whole teachings based on trying to think the right way; trying to use the mind to heal the mind; trying to think your way into solutions - oblivious that the thinking mind *is* the obstacle. These approaches just tie people in knots of overthinking.

Beyond thought, there's a whole other level of being waiting for us to access it - which is the answer we've been looking for.

Meditation: Forget what you know

The practical way to sync up with your Real Self is through the practice of *meditation*. And that's the essence of all the ideas in this book.

But don't get confused, or make that word mean something it doesn't: by meditation I simply mean doing something which gets you to drop out of thinking and sync up with your Real Self.

So much has been said about meditation, much of which has been confused with unhelpful ideas or dogmatic rules or religion. Sometimes you see someone who meditates a lot who is living a life nothing like the one you want - a really boring life - so it puts you off. Forget what you've read: meditation is really very simple. As I've said, *by meditation I simply mean doing something which gets you to drop out of thinking and sync up with your Real Self.*

Getting back to basics

Meditation is a process of focusing on something that doesn't get you thinking too much - something neutral like the breath or a consistent sound. You use the breath or sound as an anchor point so you can be tuned into your Real Self. Focusing on things you appreciate is also a way to meditate and drop from the false self (thinking) into the Real Self (being). Working out at the gym can be meditation. In fact, there are many ways to meditate into your Real Self, as you'll learn in the next section. When you practice one of the suggested ideas, after a certain amount of time, the thinking mind seems to "give up" and release you into that space of no thought; the Real Self which is who you really are. This space may be empty of mind chatter, but it's full of who you really are - instinct and intuition, passion, excitement, adventure. You won't just be peaceful in a kind of boring way - you'll be fully you; fully enjoying life as who you really are, the Real You.

When I was going through a challenging time, the image that I clung to was a vision I'd got in meditation:

In my mind's eye I saw a kaleidoscope of faces, twisted in cruelty, deception, confusion and deep fear. It was like being in one of those circus mirrors, where everything gets distorted - but it was worse than that, like shattered glass, impossible to "make right" by myself. It was all too much, overwhelming like my life at that time.

As I meditated, I felt myself being carried back from the image. It felt like "letting go". As I was slightly away from the image, like an observer, I saw all of the fragments gliding into place like a huge jigsaw puzzle in an intricate way that I could never accomplish by my own efforts or when I was too close into the drama.

And in this vision, I got how all of my trying, my thinking, my trying to sort things out had never worked. As I stepped back from the details, everything was made right. All the relationships, all the hurt, all those situations that had looked like they were ruined were all arranged back in their perfect place. I understood the importance of meditation - and how much we resist doing it - instead preferring to think our way through life and attempting to do it our way.

So if you have relationship struggles - *meditate*
Health concerns - *meditate*
Problems with your career - *meditate*

Or you are looking for the next step to take in life - *meditate*
Whatever the problem - *meditation tunes you into the solution*

Trying to "not think" doesn't work

Trying doesn't work when it comes to getting out of the mind, because it has that edge of pushing against the opposite. When you try to sleep, you can't sleep. It's the same with meditation. It's the same with "trying" to be confident (not shy) or "trying" to love yourself (rather than dislike yourself) or "trying" to think positive thoughts (not negative thoughts). It doesn't work. Try to not think of something, like the Statue of Liberty, and you'll see what I mean. It just keeps you in a cycle of overthinking. The key is to do something else. The key is to fully understand that going into thoughts looking for answers never has worked and never will work - it offers you nothing. Thoughts are the clouds that block the lighthouse of the Real Self (your source of everything). So through trial and error, experimenting with the ideas in this book, you will stop taking the bait of following the temptation of thoughts, *no matter how enticing their high drama or how interesting they seem to be.*

Being told to just "take some deep breaths" or that I should "simply relax" or "just let go" didn't work for me. We've seen that kind of bumper sticker spirituality on social media, with the endless "Don't worry, be happy" quotes that are nice ideas, but don't help you feel better when you are in a bad place - and don't change your life.

Find what works - and then do it

You know what they say: practice makes perfect. And it does. Firstly, you've got to find the right approach, then you have to do it.

It's common for people delay dropping into their Real Self. You may never feel ready to do what it takes to tune into who you are - just as you may never feel ready to get started at the gym. The thinking mind gets threatened by those things that work - that's why this false self mindset is happy for you to just *read* self-help books and do nothing. But reading alone doesn't change you, just as reading fitness books alone doesn't change your body. You will find that it's those things that you feel somehow guided to do yet have huge resistance to doing (like meditation, or going to the gym) that are often your "way" into connection. Don't wait to want to begin - *just do it.*

The importance of a daily routine

Many people have let the false self mind run their life. Like handing over the reigns of your company to the office junior, this isn't a good idea. The under-qualified and totally out of its depth thinking mechanism gets terrified and starts "blagging". And then it creates havoc. It brings the company down; it ruins your life.

People with successful lives have realised not to let this mind chatter run their life. They have learnt how to create space to allow their inner god or goddess - the Real Self - to step in and take over each day, rather than the false self "office junior". *And daily actions are almost always necessary for this to happen.*

During my research, I discovered that most people living a good life have to *do something* to deal with their mind. It's often something that they do first thing in the morning as a ritual. It's something like the practices you will find in the Quick Reference Section of this book: a workout, a meditation, an early morning jog - *Something that breaks the circuit of thinking and gives space for the Real Self to step in and take over.*

Let me share a secret with you: The Focal-point technique (otherwise known as meditation), which you will learn in the Quick Reference Section, was the practice that really did it for me when nothing else worked. After reading hundreds of books, visiting workshop after workshop and doing my own research I was still "lost at sea". My mind was a storm of thoughts and emotions. Aided and abetted by the latest "positive thinking" gimmicky technique, I was going round and round in my thoughts. And what I wanted wasn't to be found on this trail of thinking - it was in my Real Self. *In our Real Self, we are already that which we want to be.*

I committed to doing the Focal-point technique/meditation every day and, after a few months, it transformed my experience. I see this as a foundation practice to build the others upon.

WHAT TO DO RIGHT NOW

Let's begin by calling our power back

We've all been there - that feeling in the pit of our stomach when we haven't been called back by someone we care about. Or when we are jealous of someone else's body or lifestyle or career. Or when someone we like doesn't want to talk to us. Or when we don't get that job. And then we start going into all kinds of bleak thoughts. This isn't about the other person or situation - though it can seem that way. These feelings mean we have gone into mind chatter - and are searching outside ourselves for an unrecognised quality *within* us.

Thinking that a quality *you have* is in an object or person outside yourself is what I'm talking about. The fact that you feel this longing **means that this quality is deep within you and unrealised** - like buried treasure. And the pain you feel is actually this quality within yourself that you are ignoring, calling out to you. That's what the pain is: *The fact that you have the pain means this quality is within you, undiscovered, or you couldn't feel this pain.* That's all that feeling in the pit of your stomach means: you are denying a very real part of yourself that you are attempting to get from something outside of yourself. *But it's not outside of yourself, it's an unrealised part of you.*

Often, to soothe the pain we are led to seek outside ourselves even more, continuing to ignore the inner quality which is trying to get our attention. And the painful feeling gets stronger as we move away from our Real Self, falling into more and more powerlessness - and then we crave more outside of ourselves still - and this is what's known as an addiction.

So this painful feeling is very good news, even though it may not feel that way in the moment. The longing means that the quality we are looking to get from outside of ourselves is actually *within us* - or we couldn't long. The more we chase out there, the further we depart from ourselves, the worse we feel, the more we want to chase, and it's a vicious circle. Most of us have spent a lot of our lives looking for fragments of ourselves in other people, places or things. When you own that quality in yourself, your pain will stop. *Isn't that great news?*

So firstly you want to identify the quality you are longing for, and therefore the quality you need to recognise in yourself:

What do you want that you think this person/situation will give you?

For example: You really like someone who isn't responding to you the way you'd like. It could be a friend, a family member or partner.

Situation I want to happen: *(Name of person) calls me and shows me they care*

How I would feel if this situation happened:
I want to feel reassurance
I want to feel that everything is going to be OK
I want to feel honoured
I want to feel respected
I want to feel special
I want to feel confident
I want to feel secure and feel a trust about life
I want to feel loved

So you write down the situation you want to happen. In this case, you want someone to change their behaviour towards you - something you cannot control. And underneath you write the feelings you think that you will have if they were to do this. Write *"I want to feel"* in front of each feeling description.

Whatever the subject - be it body image, relationships, work situation - anything outside of yourself - you can write at the top of the page how it would ideally be if you could press a button and change the situation to anything you want. And then list the feelings you think you'd feel if this were to happen.

Doing this exercise will "wake you up" to your power and make you realise you are looking *outside* for a quality *inside*: In this example, you will realise that you do not actually want the reassuring call at all. What you want is the feeling that you think the call will give you. By doing this exercise, you will begin to realise this quality within yourself, and you will see how this situation or person's lack of providing a need was showing you where *you* could acknowledge yourself more.

Once you fulfil yourself and soothe the neediness through the exercises in this book, the best outcome for you will mirror back from life and whether they call or not, you will be happy and all will be well.

Outside situations influence us, and this is where the confusion lies. We are chasing "out there" for what is "in here". The circumstance is mirroring back where you have a "weak muscle". And, like with a weak muscle, our own sense of self requires training many times before it's strong. It's normal if the process gets you in your power for a while, and then you fall again. Just like you don't get the perfect body on the first few times at the gym, you will likely have to do this process again and again. Just writing down the outer situation you are attempting to change, and then listing the feelings you think you will get from that change, is enough to call your power back and shift you into your Real Self. After a while, you will be resilient and just not go into powerless. *It's an incredibly powerful process.*

When you become whole, complete and fulfilled, life mirrors back that you are "it". When you are feeling whole, complete and fulfilled you are at one with your Real Self, at one with your light. You aren't engulfed with mind chatter and you don't experience needing anything outside yourself to change or be different. You are in the zone and your life reflects back this perfection. But you don't care, because you are already "it". Once you realise that all you are looking for is to realise You (and you may think it's all kinds of different things "out there", but it's not) then you are ready to begin. *So let's begin.*

QUICK REFERENCE SECTION

Three levels of feeling

The following three levels contain ways to help you relax as you read through the ideas within them. Included within each level are practical suggestions you can use, right now in this moment, to feel better.

- FEELING LOW is for when you feel not very good at all: fearful, despairing, anxious, unhappy, stressed out etc - all states of overthinking.

- FEELING UNINSPIRED is for when you feel average and averagely in thoughts, perhaps a little low on energy, lacking inspiration or feeling bored.

- FEELING GOOD is for when you feel "in the zone", clear-minded and connected, to sustain this mood and take it even higher.

Which level you go to depends upon which mood you are in at that time. Just as you shift up the gears in a car in the right order (you don't jam into fifth gear immediately) - by using the right level according to the mood you are in you will be able shift into a better mood more easily, level-by-level, without trying to jump from zero to a hundred all at once. Some of the ideas you'll discover are for when you have time sitting down with a pen and paper to hand, and others are to do when you are on the go.

Magnetic thoughts

Feeling fantastic and getting "in your zone" is not as simple and straightforward as just flicking a switch. When you are in a bad mood your mind fills with similarly negative, unpleasant thoughts making it easy to just stay stuck in this mood. This is like being tuned into a miserable channel which has nothing to offer you. For example, if you feel like a failure, then you will start to remember all the times things went wrong in your life. You probably won't like the way you look in the mirror right now. On this "channel" you will probably meet people who annoy you or who don't treat you well, and your general experience will be of a harsh and miserable world. You may be drawn to taking actions which don't work for you and make things worse. All these factors ensure that you feel even more of a failure.

When you try to think your way out of one of these low moods - to use your mind to try to change (or escape from) your thoughts - things just get worse. Your mind seems to be stuck in the hopeless drama. In your desperation to "think positive" you often end up feeling even more negative and then criticise yourself for not being able to be happy. At such times the mind rarely offers ideas which will improve the situation, instead making suggestions that will help keep you stuck. For instance, the mind may suggest you stay in and isolate yourself when in such situations it is often better to go out with friends. Or the mind may encourage you to overthink things or try to jump into immediately feeling incredible when that just isn't an option right now.

So, it makes sense that when you are in a low mood, your best strategy is to step aside from the mind and take time out to regroup, much as you would in a sports game you were losing at halftime. This approach highlights the difference between frantically rummaging through junk on the "bargain basement" floor of a department store where nothing is up to your standards (overthinking), versus stepping aside and relaxing into the elevator to move up to a floor containing things (and ideas and feelings) you do like.

Accept where you are – and then distract

As strange as it sounds, the first step to escape this lower self mindset is to fully settle into and embrace it. Logically this doesn't make sense (why would we accept being somewhere we don't want to be?), but when we are able to be okay with where we are, we give up the battle with whatever's going on and automatically drop into the Real Self where the solutions we want are. This isn't about forcing anything or trying too hard; the process is gentle and easy, like breathing. It's like gently turning the dial on a radio to tune in to a clear signal. Although our knee-jerk reaction is often to struggle against where we are, it is in relaxing that solutions lie.

Letting go can seem pointless. The lower self mind thinks if we let go of the problem we'll never find the answer. Even the common dictionary definitions of words about letting go, like the word *surrender,* imply admitting defeat and staying in a terrible place. But the opposite is true. It is only when we have let go of the problem that we can find the solution. Acceptance doesn't mean dwelling on the unpleasant aspects of the situation – it means giving up the battle with the situation, which then reveals solutions and enables you to move on.

For example, recall a time when you lost something important that you really needed, like your door keys. You can search for hours and not find them. Yet when you relax and distract yourself from the need for them - perhaps you find another set of keys, or you get busy with something else - you discover they were in that pocket, or on that shelf all along.

Just begin

From the vantage point of your low moods, the mind can chatter negatives such as, "why bother", or "how is this going to work when other things haven't?" When you are in a less than good mood, the mind is not a friend. In this state the mind repeatedly turns over problems which further keeps you in this low mood. So waiting for motivational ideas to inspire you when you don't feel good is a catch-22. You are waiting for encouragement on a lower mood zone that contains only thoughts and evidence of discouragement and excuses - and so you won't find it.

The key is to turn to the appropriate level for you at this moment and go right ahead and begin, whether you feel like it or not.

Dive into the following levels and let the ideas there work for you. If you have any kind of problem at all, you will find the exercises help shift you to the place where the perfect solution awaits you. As we become more clear-minded our vision and perception also becomes clearer, and we observe things we previously didn't notice.

Change requires some effort. It is easier in some ways to just stay in the same routine. But, as you personally experience success with these techniques, you will develop a new routine you enjoy doing and using them will be almost automatic.

Each state of being has its benefits

Interestingly, each level has its own advantages and so one is actually not better than the other. When you are in clouds of overthinking and feeling low, this state is what drives your greatest evolution and so is as valid and vital as being fully connected with your Real Self. Each state of being is part of the whole process of life. Remember that wherever you are is where you are meant to be. The first stage is accepting this, knowing that whichever mood you find yourself in is okay and nothing has gone wrong. In this acceptance, you will loosen up and move closer to your natural, confident Real Self state.

Whatever you are going through at any moment is a perfect part of your journey, and exactly where you are supposed to be. It may not feel that way when you are in the middle of a difficult situation, but in time you will see that nothing went wrong. Whether you are creating evolution (and "having a good workout") in the storms of overthinking or receiving your good (and fully relaxed into your light) in your Real Self, it's all part of the process of life and it's all ok.

Shifting gears in an order that works

So, let's go over how to shift up the levels of mood again:

The Feeling Low level is for clearing our minds and floating, putting ourselves in neutral and gently beginning to loosen up.

When we visit the second stage, the Feeling Uninspired level, we begin to appreciate where we are. In this slightly better mood we can begin to recognise the benefits in any challenges we have been experiencing, or find the positive side of people we have not being getting on well with. Appreciation is the way to accept, and in acceptance we can let go.

Finally we go to the Feeling Good level where we are "in our zone". This is our natural state, where we feel ourselves the most. When we are free-flowing, clear-minded and fully at-one with our power we can feel even better by relaxing into our imagination.

Whatever the problem, there is a solution

It doesn't matter what the problem is, whether it is to do with relationships, finances, health or career issues, the answer comes when we get into our Real

Self. The shift we are looking for is not "out there" but within.

It is best to approach the following practices with no expectation. Simply try them out, do not do them to change or achieve anything. Just fully immerse yourself in the experience. You may also want to open your chosen level at random and begin reading and following the suggestions - you may find it is the perfect thing you need right now.

THREE LEVELS OF FEELING

FEELING LOW (Full on workout/resistance training mode): *Lost in overthinking, storm clouds covering the light.* Settle into where you are and what's going on. Step back from the mind. Detach and surrender. Relax into where you are.

Techniques: Focal-point technique/meditation, Deep breathing, Sound Focus technique, Point of Light technique, Shower technique, Crystal Focus technique, Power naps, Mantras, Universe List and Physical exercise.

FEELING UNINSPIRED (Moderate workout mode): *The light is slightly dimmed with overthinking. Moderate workout and moderate receiving.* Gentle distraction. Appreciate your present moment. Appreciate the life you have now.

Techniques: General Appreciation List, Specific Appreciation List, Looking for the good in where you are List, Universe List, Mantras/Affirmations and Physical exercise.

FEELING GOOD (Receiving mode): *Tuned into your confident Real Self. Receiving what your workout in the "lower levels" has created.* Follow your guidance and envision your ideal life.

Technique: Envisioning/Visualisation.

FEELING LOW

Feeling: empty, depressed, fearful, despairing, down, resentful, terrible.

Your mind is your own worst enemy in this mood and you experience few good feelings. Your repetitive thoughts keep you stuck and the more you "try" to be happy, the more miserable you seem to become. So, your solution is to step back from your mind; to detach from the mind.

When you are not feeling good the mind operates in a vicious circle, turning the same thoughts over and over in a vain attempt to discover a solution. And solutions don't ever appear in this way. You have to somehow break this circuit and create a space so you can be freed from this pattern.

In this low mood, you want to find a way to "float" rather than fighting or struggling. When you try hard to undo a knot it can sometimes tighten more, but as you take a more relaxed approach, it loosens. It's the same with the mind; floating means not engaging in arguments with the mind (a strategy that only keeps you trapped in the drama).

The letters F.E.A.R. create two phrases: *False Evidence Appearing Real,* which makes you *Forget Everything About Reality.* With fear and all those other low emotions such as despair, jealousy, insecurity and hatred, the world looks different, and everything in it seems miserable. When you are feeling low, it seems that happiness is non-existent and this bad mood will last forever. But this is an illusion; the mood will pass in time.

When you are not feeling good your mind can overthink, which frustratingly is the exact opposite approach of what will get you out of the mood. Your mind is not a friend when your feel low, going into overthinking and keeping you in the low mood. So, it is a good idea to take time to learn to step back from the mind.

Common sense informs us the best time to approach and ride a horse is not when it's rearing up and being wild. If you did, things would not go so well. Instead, you want to wait until it calms down. Then you can ride it and have an enjoyable experience. So it is with the mind trapped in repetitive thoughts: you want to "get off" the mind and wait until it calms down before you continue. This is the way you will learn and practice as you follow these words.

No matter how unusual it seems to you, the first thing is to settle into where you are right now. Your mind may be in overdrive with analysing and thinking in a desperate attempt to try to figure out solutions - but this is not the time to go into thinking. It's like being tuned into a horror movie on TV and watching it to try to find peace. Peace isn't there. Peace is on a different channel. So, to find this peace, you want to find a way to change channel to the relaxed, calm mind. When you are there, you can begin to listen within to the guidance of the Real Self that arises.

Once you loosen up, the problematic thoughts will let go of you and you will be released into the good-feeling zone: that place where what you are looking for is. As you use the ideas here, and as you wait in a relaxed "floating" way, help will arrive.

When you feel bad, the mood can sometimes feel as if it is permanent and as if it's "game over". But this isn't real: relief is just moments away. The techniques described below will help you to shift from the overthinking channel to the Real Self channel where better feeling insights and experiences reside. These techniques have been thoroughly tried-and-tested. Many people have used them to feel better, and they will work for you too.

What to do: Firstly, make peace with where you are

- Be ok with where you are. Of course this sounds ridiculous to you right now because your mind wants to kick and scream against the bad feelings and move to being happy immediately. But there is no rush. You are supposed to be here. Nothing has gone wrong. This experience is evolving your life to a better place, though you can't see that yet. Embrace this bad feeling rather than arguing with it. Like a storm coming over, you want to stay within yourself and wait while it passes through - and it will pass through.

- Like a rip tide that's got hold of you, when you're in the middle of a problem and your mind is swirling with negative thoughts, your best bet is to go with the "current" of thoughts. Fighting them or trying to change them into "happy ones" is like struggling against a powerful tide: you will exhaust yourself. But as you relax into them, in time they will pass as you "drop into" your Real Self.

- Fighting against where you are doesn't work. Think of a spider's web and how with every struggle you would become more trapped in it. You have to fully give yourself to the "web" of negative thoughts to drop through them. Or think of being overboard in the ocean. Your best chance of survival is to relax and float, even though your mind wants to tell you to kick and scream and panic - or even try to feel "perfectly fine", when that isn't possible. *Relax into your thoughts. Breathe into them.* Don't struggle and fight them. Slow down and deepen your breathing instead.

- There is incredible power in making peace with the storms. The turmoil has created a huge solution and as you find a way to not resist, positive change will arise. In the middle of these dark times you think you've got to "do something right now" but instead, relax into the pain rather than going into thoughts. This is enough. The power of the situation has created the answer. You don't have to think about it - relax and be gently brought into the solutions.

- You may be tempted to work on a problem, or try to fix it, or try to "think better thoughts" whilst in this low mood - but don't. Tell yourself you are relaxing now. When you feel terrible, if you try to immediately jump to feeling great, you often don't make the jump. So take this time to relax, however long this takes, and then you can move to the Feeling Uninspired or Feeling Good levels and use the techniques they suggest.

- When in a low mood, we often fixate on a problem, turning it over and over again in our minds. We think that if we do this long enough we will figure out a solution. But the solution exists in a different place to the problem. We must relax into and then ease off the subject - let loose of the problem so that the solution can come.

Nothing has gone wrong

- It's okay to feel less than good; in fact, it's a necessary part of life. When we are in the greatest pain, we are being worked on by Life - and "working out" our best life in the most powerful way. It is in our darkest times that we evolve the most, and for the better, as the expression "challenges make you stronger" explains. And so you may need this particular thought cycle you are currently having to evolve into something amazing. You are where you are, and where you are supposed to be. It's just weights at the gym, building muscle.

- This is a time to snuggle up with yourself and settle into the calm at the centre of the storm. You want to say to yourself "perhaps life is preparing me for something great", and "I am ok where I am - I am supposed to be here". Often when you don't feel good what you are actually experiencing is the evolution of positive new things; being shunted out of a rut, perhaps, and back onto your path. The light you are looking for is right here beside you: imagine your Real Self embracing you.

It's going to be ok

- When you don't feel good it's easy to have thoughts like, "this doesn't work", or "what's the point?" Don't take these thoughts personally - this is simply what everyone's mind does on the lower level. Let the thoughts be.

- Sometimes however, you may buy into these thoughts and be "taken down" by them, and that's okay too. In these times of feeling low, it can take a real effort to make ourselves use the tools outlined here, even though we may have proved to ourselves again and again that they work. Your mind in this mood may suggest all kinds of approaches that will not work, most commonly to "keep on thinking" in order to change your mood. By now you have probably tried these false suggestions enough times to know that they don't work. But this realisation does not always stop us buying into these thoughts - so accept yourself whatever you do.

- The lower level mind may also suggest things like "I shouldn't be feeling bad", or even make you feel scared of how stressful thoughts might negatively affect you. Instead remind yourself that "negativity" is sometimes necessary and is also more than alright; it's a springboard to better things. Perhaps you should be feeling this way now - because you are. There is no rush to quickly move through the bad feeling. It is part of your journey to create a great life for yourself.

- This lower level mind chatter may also tell you to resist being where you are and suggest you try to kick it away. This is not helpful. Instead, fully relax into where you are right now. Again, it's like being in the spider's web: the more you resist, the more you will become entangled. If you can fully be with this storm of thoughts in this moment then eventually the thoughts will let you go. You may even want to see this mind chatter like a tough personal trainer who is trying to bring out the best in you by pushing you further.

This too shall pass

- Patience is a good thing to have right now, because your mind may be trying to tell you "things will never change". That's just one of the many unhelpful things the mind says when you're not feeling good. Remember though, things *are* changing for the better, even as you read these words. Remember to take deep breaths, slowly inhaling and exhaling as you read these words.

- Be reassured. Everyone's mind works a similar way in the lower moods - you are not alone. As so many have repeated over the centuries: "This too shall pass". Everything does change for the better, despite what the mind may be telling you.

Soothe yourself with phrases such as "This too shall pass. I have felt terrible before and felt "finished" and I came through it. I have been here before and got through it, and know I will again. Everything is working out. I should be feeling this way right now, because I am. In this moment I am powerfully creating solutions. Beyond this mind lies the mind (the Real Mind) that I want. Things will get better".

- You will want to try to feel good right this second, but remember: you don't want to "try" at this point. Be still, float and wait to be raised "by the elevator" onto a higher level. Hammering at the "happy door" will not cause it to open; it will just stay jammed shut.

- Trying to get out of your mood may feel stressful right now. The door will open by itself, like a lock gate on a canal when the water has reached the right level. When you are relaxed the door opens at the right time. This waiting requires patience, as it would waiting on a canal boat for the lock to open as you watch the water slowly rise or fall.

Creating space or a clearing: Focal-point technique

Before going forward with your day, you want to make sure you are synced-up with your Real Self. This is where the Focal-point technique comes in. This approach to meditation is an exercise where we step back from our physical senses and our mind chatter, and allow ourselves to be re-tuned to our calm inner nature, back to being ourselves and feeling good again.

Think of the pit lane in Formula One racing, the place where the driver pulls over and sits back while the mechanics change tyres and retune the car. In the Focal-point technique, our mind is the car and we, the driver, take a backseat and relax whilst the mechanics do the rest.

The thing with the mind is when you decide to clear it by turning away from your problems, or forgetting something, it starts thinking exactly what you don't want it to think about. So, one way to do this is to turn the mind *toward* something, like a consistent sound or your breathing, rather than away from something. Regard meditation as a sanctuary to enter into, rather than a panic room to escape from your problems.

The Focal-point technique creates a clearing, a space in which to allow connection with your Real Self. In the process of going to sleep, all you can do is prepare the surroundings and then sleep takes you. No one can clearly explain how you go to sleep. It is the same with meditation; you follow some steps and guidance, create an atmosphere and then meditation just happens.

To begin with, 15 to 20 minutes is a good length of time, although you may wish to stay in the process for longer once you are familiar with it. A key thing to remember is trying too hard to meditate won't work, just as trying desperately to go to sleep doesn't work. As you relax into it, the process will take over.

As you step aside from the chattering stream of thoughts with your focus, problematic knots in your life are untangled and untied. You can't think your way out of a problem, but meditation releases you into the Real Self where answers can be discovered. Often the lower level mind loudly and frantically chatters away like a know-it-all, whilst at the same time the calm quiet voice of the Real Self offers accurate guidance. Meditation allows you to step away from the nonsense mental chatter and instead listen to the calm quiet voice of truth.

Sometimes your mind is particularly wild or upset and you may find it too difficult to sit down and be still. When the mind is agitated in this way, it's a good idea to do something else before attempting to meditate. It is better to first practice the deep breathing exercise described below, for example. Once the mind has settled a little then you can begin to meditate.

Physical exercise as a preparation for meditation

Moving your body is a great preparation for the Focal-point technique. As you get the body moving, the mind will calm down. The increased breathing and use of your muscles brought about by exercise is one of the best ways to move away from obsessing over a subject. The more strenuous the exercise is, your muscles will be engaged and the deeper your breathing will become, so the more beneficial the exercise is as a distraction. Intense exercise demands your focus. In this focused state you will solidly "drop in" to your Real Self; that self that doesn't think, it just *is*.

In my own life, when I woke up in the mornings I used to go straight into thoughts - the same self-destructive thoughts I had experienced most days for about ten years before. So instead, I threw myself into push ups which "changed the channel". So just after waking, I'd do several sets of 20 push ups. Then I'd be clear-minded enough to begin the Focal-point technique of meditation.

So find your exercise - and then do it. You may not feel like it - but just do it. (But remember not to overdo it).

WHAT TO DO RIGHT NOW

How to meditate with the Focal-point technique

So sit down. You could sit on a cushion on the floor or on a chair. You want to be comfortable but alert.

Close your eyes. Find a point of focus, such as a consistent sound that doesn't activate your mind too much. For example, you could focus on the sound of a fan or the sound of consistent traffic in the background. It's perfectly normal for your thoughts to get louder and more convincing - whether they are suggesting other more "fun" things to do, or fearful thoughts, or anything at all. Don't go with the temptation to follow these thoughts, and come back to the sound, as boring as it may seem to be. Your mind needs to be "fed" and may get furious when you don't feed it with thoughts. So it's normal if it goes wild when you first start meditating. Chasing thoughts is exciting, so we need to find an equally dynamic replacement. We want to focus on that consistent sound like we were holding tight to a hand glider flying so high that we do not have the luxury of losing our grip and wandering off into thoughts. We want to focus on the sound like it's serious business - fully give ourselves to the sound.

Don't "try to" meditate - it doesn't work

In truth, your Real Self is always in a state of clear-minded meditation - so it's about *joining with* or *relaxing into* your Real Self, not "trying to be connected". As I've said "trying to" keeps us in thoughts - and out of the clarity of our Real Self.

Deep breathing: regroup and reconnect

- Deep breathing is a way to drop into your Real Self. As you breathe deeply and slowly, your mood elevates and you drop out of mind chatter.

- As the deliberate deep breathing physically expands and loosens the body, it also loosens the mind. So often our mind becomes tight and feels constricted when we obsess about something negative. At the same time we feel this tightness in our body. So breathing loosens everything. Filling your body with breath, like a hot air balloon, elevates you to better feelings and a better experience. Deep breathing lightens you up.

WHAT TO DO RIGHT NOW

Deep breathing

Begin by getting comfortable and sitting upright so your back is straight. First exhale fully through the mouth or nose. Now inhale deeply through your nose so you first fill the belly with air. Make sure your stomach rises as you inhale. Continue the inhalation to then fill the chest. Make sure your chest rises as you continue inhaling. Now, exhale fully through your mouth or nose allowing the chest to fall, followed by pulling the stomach inward to help push out all of the air. You may want to place one hand on the stomach and one hand on the chest to maintain the depth and rhythm of breathing; to show you that your body is expanding with the inhale, and contracting with the exhale and to show that the breath moves firstly into the stomach, then the chest and exhales firstly from the chest area, and then the stomach, in this order.

Before you start your deep breathing practice you may like to set a timer on your phone or on a clock in front of you. Breathe in for fifteen seconds, and then exhale for fifteen seconds. This means two full breaths per minute. Remember not to strain at all or overdo it. If you find yourself struggling, take more breaths per minute until you feel relaxed. Then return to the two breaths per minute again.

As you become more practiced, you can come down to one breath per minute, initially practicing for three minutes, with three full breaths in and three full exhalations. Or feel free to continue for as long as it takes to calm your mind. Once you feel comfortable and accustomed to the deep breathing, you can extend the practice to breathing into the body. Let me explain: Move your attention down to your feet and let them relax. To help the feet relax fully imagine the pores opening, and as you breathe imagine your feet breathing with you, in and out. Now move your attention to your ankles, and repeat the same technique here, continue moving into the whole of your body, visualising the skin "breathing" in and out as you do.

Instead of seeing breathing as hard work, focus on the enjoyment of the breath coming in and out. Breathe not just once or twice - but twenty times or more. Keep on going until you are "airlifted" out of your turbulent mind. Through frequent practice, you will become good at the deep breathing rhythm and may no longer need to time yourself. The key is to give the breath more authority than your thoughts - give it your total 100% focus like it was your one chance at success. Hold to the breath, focusing beyond the clouds of thoughts and allow the breath to pull you back to centre.

WHAT TO DO RIGHT NOW

Sound Focus technique

Wherever you are, begin to listen for a consistent sound in the background. This may be the sound of a fan, the engine of a vehicle like a train that you're on, traffic on a distant road etc. If you are out walking in the town or city you can listen for a consistent urban sound, or if you are walking in the countryside, listen for a consistent sound in nature. As you notice your mind wandering away from the sound bring your attention back to this consistent sound. Breathe into the atmosphere of sound. It's another anchor to calm the mind.

Point of Light technique

An alternative to listening for a sound is to move your attention to an imagined light high above you. Visualise an orb or a point of light shining consistently, like a pilot light or a star. Rest your attention gently on this point of light in your mind's eye, and keep coming back to it as you are tempted to go into thoughts. You can also combine this with the Sound Focus technique above, imagining that the consistent sound you have identified is emanating from the point of light you are focusing on. You may want to imagine a column of light and hold to this column. Breathe into the light. Give it your undivided focus.

Shower technique

Sit under a warm shower and feel the soothing of the water. Move your attention to the sound of the water, close your eyes and turn your attention inwards. Listen to the sound of the falling water and feel it on your body, move your attention within, relaxing and letting yourself go. You can also use the Sound Focus and Point of Light techniques whilst you sit here, allowing the water to soothe you back into connection.

Crystal Focus technique

Imagine an atom: with your Real Self as the nucleus, and thoughts as electrons spinning around it. Imagine this nucleus like a bright diamond crystal. Come to centre. Like a snow globe, settle, allowing the thoughts to fall, leaving you with a clear vision.

There's a TV program called *The Crystal Maze*. Towards the end of the program, there is a dome where people have to catch gold or silver bits of tin foil which are blown into the dome. It's kind of like a large snow globe, but instead of snow there are shiny bits of foil.

Imagine that - but we are going to do the exact opposite. We are going to stay within - and all those "silver and gold foil" thoughts which are desperately trying to get our attention - we are going to leave them be.

So close your eyes, and visualise a point of light in the centre of a huge globe. Become close to this nucleus. Stay in the centre and allow the thoughts to be, leave them be. Leave these electron-like thoughts spinning around you and come back to centre. Unlike the program, we leave the shiny bits of foil to fly all over the place and focus fully on our centre.

The lower self mind has been described as a "magpie" - going for shiny bits of foil that sparkle but get us nowhere. So in this technique we are not going to be fooled by the temptation of thoughts. We are going to stay in our centre.

If we really get in touch with our feelings, we will feel a "dip" in our mood when we go for the thoughts. This is our guidance telling us that we've just separated from our Real Self perspective. Come back to the "crystal" nucleus centre.

What gets us to go into thoughts is habit, and also that we think there's some benefit in doing this. There isn't. We need not encourage our thought process. Instead, let us make our effort toward keeping centred in our Real Self.

Turn toward the Inner Truth within

When you are in a low place your physical senses will mirror back to you where you are. That is why constantly checking your image in the mirror is a nightmare when you don't feel attractive. So, do not "check in" with the senses so much. Turn within by doing one of these techniques instead.

WHAT TO DO RIGHT NOW

Put on music you like or a relaxation audio. You could play music that feels good - and have a lie down. *Relax, Release and Let go* is a relaxation audio specially designed to comfort and uplift you back to peace and calm again. It's available from www.michaeljames.be.

WHAT TO DO RIGHT NOW

Power nap: A short sleep to reset your mood

Sometimes, if you are totally tangled in thoughts, it's time for a reboot - like on a computer when the system crashes. If all else fails and you want a way to refresh and "reset", set a timer for ten minutes with the intention of a short sleep or nap. As you lie in bed, feel yourself in your imagination holding yourself, wrapping your arms around yourself as you would someone you loved. Feel the bed embracing you as you relax into it and get comfortable.

There is nothing wrong with sleeping in short bursts in the day no matter what the lower level mind might tell you. My mind used to tell me, "You must be really messed up to have to sleep in the day", so I delayed this technique. But it's a far better use of time than stumbling on through your day feeling terrible. In fact, taking a nap can be a great way to reboot your mood completely. (However, sleeping for longer than fifteen to twenty minutes may leave you feeling not so good and disorientated when you wake.)

Mantras: Freedom from the mind

A mantra is simply a statement or phrase you repeat, usually many times. The word mantra means "to free from the mind". By focusing on the repetition of these words - which you can repeat out loud or silently - mantras are a distraction for a wandering mind. Like so many of the techniques described in the Feeling Low level of this book, such as deep breathing or Point of Light or Sound Focus, repeating a mantra turns your attention away from the lower level mind chatter. The mantra repetition creates space to hear the softer, loving truth of the Real Self mind.

It doesn't matter so much which mantra you use, but often words in another language are good because they won't activate your mind to think about the meaning too much. If you do use an English language mantra, you want to choose one safely off the subject of the issue and one that brings you comfort. For example, you wouldn't repeat "I am confident and beautiful" if you were in the middle of an attack of feeling unattractive and shy. Nor would you recite positive statements about your home if you were feeling particularly worried about your living situation.

You also wouldn't repeat "I am in a wonderful relationship" if your mind is knotted up with relationship issues. I have found that when you are deeply in a problem, saying words on the subject of the problem only amplifies it. Your solution is to be found when you stop thinking of the problem. And you stop thinking of the problem by focusing on something else, which is what all of these practical ideas are about. But see what works for you: you will find what soothes you.

Choose mantras that are easy to repeat, on subjects you find comforting or don't care so much about at the moment, and totally "off subject" of your problem. Find words that relax you and don't get you into overthinking.

A more dynamic point of focus

In the Focal-point technique, the equivalent of the mantra words is the consistent sound that you return to again and again. Sometimes, using a word or statement to repeat over and over can be a more dynamic focal point, giving your mind something more tangible to hold onto.

WHAT TO DO RIGHT NOW

Suggested Mantras

If you are tangled in thoughts and the pain that comes with that, you want to face exactly where you are. For example, if you are in the middle of emotional pain use the words "Thank you for this pain." This sounds a strange choice of words, but it will get you to embrace the pain rather than fight it (and fighting it keeps you stuck there and makes matters worse). Repeat these words over and over. You may want to lie down in bed, repeating these words and settling in for a short "power nap" in the daytime or do this process if you are awoken in the middle of the night in anxiety. Use "Thank you for..." whatever the situation you are experiencing is, and repeat until you relax.

When you are feeling slightly better:

A suggestion to begin with could be simply the words "Thank you". This short phrase acknowledges that everything is a blessing in disguise. Or perhaps this one, by personal development teacher Louise L. Hay: "All is well. Everything is working out for my highest good. Out of this situation only good will come. I am safe." You don't have to *feel* the meaning of the words as you repeat them, just simply repeat the phrase again and again.

Whenever a difficult, challenging situation comes up in your mind, repeat these words over and over until you are distracted away from the bad feeling.

With mantras, people are often instructed to repeat the statements until peace comes. Practicing mantra recitation with other people can deepen the meditation experience. A suggestion: When you are repeating your mantra, with your eyes closed, you may want to see the mantra's words on a screen in front of you, filling your vision in your mind's eye - it's another point of focus.

You will discover which particular mantras work for you.

A good workout

When difficulties come up, remind yourself, "This is a good workout. I'm meant to be here right now". The good thing about tension is it creates new experiences, and it is these challenges that sculpt the best of our future. So, relax into the tension. Accept it and feel it fade away.

Use the various techniques described above to settle into and unhook from the mind. And then, when you can, distract yourself until you relax into the calm of the Real Self.

Don't "try" to be happy from a place of unhappiness - it's almost guaranteed to fail. Such a strategy is merely pushing away and fighting against the state of being you don't want, and makes moving away from it virtually impossible. Busying yourself with all the techniques offered here instead will get you focused and leave less room for worrisome thoughts.

As you feel a little bit better...

Universe List

Drawing up a Universe List is a useful technique for clearing your mind, and reminding yourself of your priorities for the day. When your mind is clear it is amazing how you discover new ideas, people and places to provide you with the solutions you want.

First, take a piece of paper and draw a margin down the left hand side of the page and a margin across the top. At the top of the left hand side write "Me", and on the right hand side write the best word for you that symbolises something to hand over your problems. You may want to call it the Real Self, Life, the Creator, my Higher Power, God or even "angels". Whatever feels good for you. The list will look like this:

Me	Universe/Life/Real Self
Meditation	Sort out my life
Exercise	Sort out my relationships
Deep breathing	Sort out my home
	Take away my problems and replace them with solutions
	Help me feel safe and know that everything is working out for me
	Get me into my "Real Self"
	Show me how to make peace with where I am and who I am
	Help me to stand tall
	Show me the blessings in this experience, right now
	Replace my insecurity/neediness with confidence
	Help me surrender
	Connect me with good-feeling thoughts and feelings

On the left hand side write down what *you* are going to do that will allow you to relax and be tuned into your Real Self. In the example above are meditation (Focal-point technique), physical exercise and deep breathing, with more suggestions to be found throughout this level. You may also add any other things you already do to relax and get in the zone. For instance gardening, swimming or other sports can all be effective ways to "get you in". So write down whatever you personally do that works for you.

On the other side of the margin, write down everything you'd like to hand over to the Universe/Life/Real Self e.g. all your troubles in the form of a request. Just throw them all out on the right side. Don't hide anything - all those "shameful" parts of yourself you might not have told anyone - just throw them out there. Or write down phrases such as: "Bring my body into perfect alignment, now", "Allow me to be confident", "Bring me peace", or "Get me to fully relax". You may also want to ask the Universe to "Bring me new good-feeling ideas", or "Arrange something for me which feels good". Or any loved ones or relationships on your mind - just hand it all over: "Sort out my relationship with Jenny", "Give me a new perspective on my relationship with Justin".

The key with the wording is to write down whatever feels good to you. It's important to remember that you are not trying to believe these phrases or statements. Your job is to write them down: "throw them" onto the right hand side to get them out of your mind and into the hands of Life or the Creator or whatever you want to call it - and then get on with the tasks on your side of the margin.

You can also write down requests for others, for example, "Bring Mark his ideal job" or "Encourage Nicola to feel confident and great about herself" or "Watch over Stephen and help him find his way".

Once you have finished your list, it is done. Rip it up and throw it away. Your task now is to do what you wrote you are going to do on the left hand side of the list.

Your work is not to overthink or figure anything out; it's to offload your problems and questions, and then use the techniques you committed to, which you have written in the left hand column. Remind yourself you've delegated, and now get on with your practice and your life.

For every problem that exists, there is always a solution. But you often can't see it when you're in the problem. As you relax and distract, when the time is right the answers and the good feelings will make themselves known to you without your effort. The right people will speak the right words to you; something will definitely happen. The things on the right hand side of the Universe List will start to happen too, but there is no need for you to wonder how. Just get on with your side of the list.

After the storm

What do you feel like after a really intense workout at the gym, or a full day's hike in the countryside? You relax with a cup of tea perhaps or a night out with friends, and feel relief and satisfaction that you've accomplished something. You appreciate that you now get to rest as your body rebuilds and renews itself even better than before.

You also feel like this after the storm of a negative mood has passed. It feels like you've gone through a great workout. Nothing has gone wrong like nothing went wrong at the gym. Now you can settle into the knowing that you have evolved to a new, better place. You have done your work and now it is time to rest. Quieten your mind and listen for new ideas and insights as you feel good again.

FEELING UNINSPIRED

Feeling: low on energy, lack of inspiration, bored.

There is always something to appreciate, right where we are. Actually there are many things we can appreciate. The only real power of choice we have is over our attitude, to appreciate - or to go into thinking and complain about something. That seemingly tiny choice can mean the difference between success and failure in all areas of our life. This sounds like a simplistic idea - and it certainly simplifies life.

Often our excuse for not appreciating the things which are already going well in our life comes from the mistaken idea that we must instead spend our time analysing problems in order to solve them. But you can rise above all problems, where you'll discover solutions (and everything else that you want) by deliberately looking for things to appreciate. In fact, when any problem or "need" comes to mind, quickly distracting onto a success in your life - something which is working - takes your mind from the problem and effortlessly moves you into the "answer zone" and makes you feel good now. Of course, this takes a little effort, because it is easier for the mind to keep on running in the direction it's already going in - but this little commitment to do the techniques you'll read here will change your life in extraordinary ways. (However if appreciation is too difficult a state to access, refer to the Feeling Low level instead).

Appreciation literally means to recognise the full value of something, and also means "to increase". When you look for things to appreciate, you seem to discover more and more things to feel good about and before long, this "glass half full" attitude becomes a habit and your life keeps getting better. With your focus on appreciation you can feel good even before your dreams come true, without anything outside of yourself needing to change. When you dwell on the successes you already have in your life, you elevate your mood and begin to realise you are closer to fulfilling your dreams than you believed as new thoughts, ideas and new ways of looking at things come into view. Practicing looking for what's already good in your life will also give you a good-feeling space to go to if problems arise and threaten to ruin your mood.

Dwell on what's working in your life

You can't appreciate and think at the same time. Appreciation opens the door to your Real Self.

The mind thinks it needs to focus on problems to solve them, so it does that, constantly. This does nothing to solve them.

Look right in front of you. Is there a rug on the floor? A particular grain of wood on the table? A cup of tea, the ingredients of which have been prepared by someone else, in a mug that was made by someone else? There are many people and things to appreciate right here and now. A straightforward Appreciation List takes you straight into the zone - out of thinking and into the fulfilment of your Real Self.

Appreciation connects you with You

You are always your Real Self underneath the storm of thoughts. You can never really stray off your path, as your Real Self (your inner god or goddess) always walks, steadfastly feeling like God's gift; confident, beautiful and self-assured. So no matter how you feel, somewhere within, you are constantly shining and becoming even more of who you are.

Appreciation allows you to become your Real Self, opening the door to solutions, and getting us to drop out of our thinking mind and into who we really are.

WHAT TO DO RIGHT NOW

General Appreciation List

First take a piece of paper, or a page in a notepad, and begin writing a list of things that are easy to like, on subjects that are not problematic for you. For example, if your career is going well and is an area of life that is easy for you to appreciate then begin with that. Write down what you appreciate in your work situation. For example, "I love how good my work makes me feel. I love the people I work with, such as Sam and his sense of humour, and I love how he always makes me tea in the morning". Begin, and watch how more ideas on the subject come to you.

You can follow this with writing down your past and current successes and accomplishments on all subjects. List compliments and good experiences you have had, special people in your life and talents and good qualities you know you have. For instance, "I love that I won Salesperson of the Year last year", or "As I was walking down the high street last week I loved how that guy smiled at me". Or "I loved it when Sarah said what a great friend I am".

WHAT TO DO RIGHT NOW

Specific Appreciation List

You can focus in on particular areas or people in your life, and look for the things you like about them. Write headings such as: Body image, Romantic relationships, Family relationships and Career and/or Life purpose etc. Start by bringing to mind a certain situation or person, for example a family member or your boss at work. Write a list of good things about them, or good things they have done for you. It doesn't matter if the good thing was ten minutes ago or ten years ago; appreciation is appreciation.

For example, "I love the fun we had when my friend Eric visited and we went to the art gallery," Or, "I love how my mum buys in all the food I like when I visit", or "My boss complimented me on that job I did", or "I like my colleague's sense of humour and his fashion sense".

Looking for the good in problems

Sometimes we're afraid to look at our problems - those parts of ourselves we don't like - and so we end up trying to ignore or deny them. Although this book explains the power of turning away from your problems, resisting or denying problems is a very different thing that does not work. When people "try not to think" about their problems, they obsess about them; but their problems remain, like the elephant in the room. Try not to think of the Statue of Liberty and you'll see what I mean.

This technique isn't about searching for problems, it's about reworking your attitude around those problems you can't seem to forget about no matter how hard you try. Some subjects, such as romantic relationships or body image can play frequently on our minds. We're endlessly reminded of them by conversations, advertisements, music lyrics and our own mind. So for situations that you can't distract yourself from, your best option is to change your perspective about them. To let them go, you want to look for the good in them.

This is difficult for the thinking mind to understand: "Why would I appreciate something I don't want?" But fighting our problems hasn't worked. So why not do the opposite?
When we look for the good wherever we may be, this is where transformation happens: we then realise that our problems are not problems at all, but opportunities. This is not an intellectual process but an emotional and practical one.

To let go or surrender from anything, you want to *embrace* where you are. As I mentioned before, what you resist persists, because when you fight against something it sticks to you like glue as long as your attention remains on it. It's like being in a vehicle stuck in mud with your foot on the accelerator, wheel-spinning and moving nowhere. Appreciating where you are right now allows you to relax and pause, freeing you to go forward.

As you learn to look for the good in all experiences, even your negative thinking and bad moods, you will leave behind anything that isn't the best for you. You will withdraw from the problematic subject, the knots that bind you to issues will be undone, and you will flow unhindered. When you appreciate the good in your problems you set yourself free.

WHAT TO DO RIGHT NOW

Looking for the good in where you are List

If there are problems on your mind, it's time to add them to your Appreciation List. Write down the issue, what it is and perhaps also how you think it affects you, and then see if you can find some good things within it.

For example, "Not liking my body and being obsessed about it". Good things about not liking my body may include: "It has encouraged me to join a gym which I really enjoy", or "It encouraged me to buy a really good book which led to happiness in other areas of my life and got me to start meditating which has been beneficial", or "There are many people who have gone from feeling unattractive to feeling incredibly attractive", or "My strong desire for improvement has evolved success on this subject", or "I believe life is on my side so everything that happens to me is good, so this has to be good and I will discover that knowing". Good things about the obsessiveness may include: "This intensity around me is incredibly attractive when used to focus on good-feeling things. All successful, charismatic people are intense", or "This pain forced me to surrender and get into meditation and relaxation".

Good things about being rejected: "It has shown me where I reject myself and where I have a weak muscle I can train in this area. Perhaps this person is not right from me, and Life is making space for someone else. This situation should have happened because it did".

Good things about being lonely: "I should be feeling lonely because I am. Everyone feels lonely sometimes, and this feeling passes. This loneliness is evolving me to an incredible social life and an incredible intimate, fulfilling relationship".

Good things about losing my temper: "It shows I have passion. Everyone, including babies, feel angry and frustrated sometimes. Babies quickly forget about it and so will I".

Feeling bored? This emotion can be hard to understand as it feels like a non-emotion. What boredom actually is, however, is a lot of subtle low-level mind chatter clouding your connection, often so "low volume" that it gives the illusion of stagnancy or non-emotion. The frustration of boredom actually comes from an endless resistance to being bored, so the answer is to embrace it. Have a go at writing down a list of appreciation about being bored. For example, "Being bored means I've got no big problems". Repeating statements or mantras (see "Mantras" later in this level) will also drop you out of the overthinking state of boredom and bring you into the excitement and interest of the Real Self.

WHAT TO DO RIGHT NOW

Universe List

Take a new sheet of paper or page in your notebook. Surrender anything that is on your mind (including anything you might want or want to change in your life) by writing it down on the right hand side of the list. Then write down the actions you are going to commit to in order to sync up with your Real Self on the left hand side. The list will look like this:

Me	Universe/Life/Real Self
Meditation	Thank you for my confidence
Gym	Help me feel confident about my body
Appreciation	Sort out my relationship
	Thank you for my new job.
	Show me the best place for me to live
	Take away my boredom and replace it with excitement
	Surround me only with people who love and respect me
	Keep me steadfastly anchored in my Real Self
	Bring me a dynamic new hobby

One way to use the Universe List is to write down something like, "Thank you for my perfect body", or "Thank you for my confidence". To help you decide how you phrase what you write, let's consider a boss making a request of one of his work team. He might phrase it like, "Please could you finish this project", or alternatively, "Thank you for finishing the project". Which statement do you feel is the most definite and the most certain and the one that shows the most faith and trust? The second one is more declarative and would allow the boss to walk away trusting that the request has been fulfilled. But this is just a suggestion: it's the feeling that the wording evokes that matters. The words themselves are not so important.

Further examples include: "Help me feel beautiful", or "Help me feel wealthy", or "Sort out this relationship with (insert name here)", or "Thank you for helping me feel successful", or "Bring me more success", or "Thank you for helping me feel loved", or "Thank you for getting me to feel fully fulfilled, whole and complete right now".

Mantras & Affirmations to ramp up the feeling

Mantras are statements you repeat over and over to "drop in" to your Real Self. They give your mind a "toy" to play with. But unlike those in the previous Feeling Low level, this time we will choose statements about dreams that haven't happened yet. We will write these mantras down in the present tense. Some people call these types of mantras affirmations, which means "to make firm", because a by-product of saying the mantra is that it reinforces your mind with a new way of looking at life, which keeps you out of overthinking.

Mantras can be a distraction away from a wandering mind and also bring relief and excitement to a bored mind. They also provide a way into a feeling of excited anticipation through their constant repetition, although you are not actually "trying to" believe or expect anything. This is an important point: people sometimes say mantras or affirmations when they are frightened of the subject they are focusing on. They fearfully try to change their reality by making themselves believe something different about the same subject.

If you feel fearful in this way, then it is too big a leap to take at this time. When you feel down or defeated, saying, "My life is wonderful" will probably just backfire on you. "But my life isn't wonderful", your lower level "inner critic" voice will argue back intensely. So, before you can move on to saying mantras about specific subjects you need to feel okay first, and not in a current mental battle with that subject.

If you are in a low mood or if it feels like you are saying the statement to try to make something happen "out there" or to fix your life, discontinue. If it doesn't feel good when you repeat these mantra statements, stop. Do a practice from the Feeling Low level instead. Remember you are doing this practice to relax into your Real Self - that's all. When you are too tightly caught up in a problem, doing mantras on the subject of that problem can be like trying to jam a car straight into a high gear from stationary. It's simply too big a jump and it will bring more frustration. But if the statement brings you peace and makes you feel good and relaxed, continue. Through trial and error you will find the statements that work for you. Keep on saying the mantra. It may take a few times or a few hundred times of repetition to really let loose of thoughts and begin feeling better. Some people don't repeat mantras for long enough to see their mood consistently change.

WHAT TO DO RIGHT NOW

Examples of mantras you can use

Here are a few general statements you can use as mantras: "I am confident and beautiful", or "I live in a beautiful house in (my favourite area)", or "I am an abundant and successful person", or "I have a great relationship with (name the person here)". Select whichever mantra appeals to you and feels good to you and repeat it over and over, either under your breath or in your mind.

The key is to choose a sentence or two that feels good and begin repeating it immediately. Not just a few times, but for ten or twenty or thirty minutes, however long it takes to shift your mood - which may be hundreds of times. Whenever you feel less than fantastic, simply return to repeating your mantra until you return to feeling good again. The mind may prefer to languish in boredom rather than "do the work" - so a little effort is required. Keep up and you will be kept up!

It doesn't really matter what the words of the mantra mean specifically. Because you are repeating the mantra statement mostly for distraction you are not meant to ponder, or think about the meaning. You are not saying the statement to change anything, or to make anything that hasn't happened happen. Repeating your mantra is a distraction from your issues and works like a meditation, to drop you out of the clouds of overthinking and into your Real Self.

However, at the same time, the words of the mantra do gently introduce an idea to your mind which becomes a new idea to focus on as opposed to your previous worries. It's not that you "need" this new belief, but the new messages knock the old thoughts patterns to the side like a winning boule ball.

Remember to choose a subject that isn't problematic for you: you want to speak a mantra about your dream relationship when you are either already in it, or you don't really care/need it. If you care too much about relationships and feel "needy" around them - choose another subject. Choose a subject you already have some belief in - for example if you sometimes feel quite wealthy, "I am wealthy and living the life of my dreams" won't be too much of a jump. Your feelings will tell you if you are stretching too far.

While you are travelling, either in a vehicle or on foot you can try repeating your chosen mantra over and over. This repetition will help prevent your focus wandering off into places and moods you don't want to go to. The phrase that "the devil makes work for idle hands" means that when we are not focusing, we can veer into thoughts and and get lost. A mantra gives the lower self mind a "toy" to play with and keeps us out the way of thoughts and anchored in our Real Self.

Other ideas

Helping others to feel good can also get you out of your own problems of thinking and connect you with your Real Self. What you give, you instantly receive in the form of a good feeling.

You can also put on some music that makes you feel good, or do physical exercise that you enjoy.

FEELING GOOD

Feeling: "in the Zone", clear-minded, free-flowing, whole and complete, totally fulfilled and exhilarated about life, light and free of thoughts.

You feel good, so now it's time to increase your enjoyment of life even more.

The practice of Envisioning (or "visualisation") is best used when you are already feeling good. Envisioning dispels any longing or desires for something in the future to be different by giving you the feeling of achieving your dreams right now. This technique is about opening to ideas and enjoying the end results of your dreams without having to wait for anything "out there" to change.

Envisioning helps you enjoy life fully right now, as it heightens your mood in a way that mere appreciation of what you already have cannot.

Another great thing about envisioning is it creates a mental space, like a vivid memory, to which you can return to again and again at a later date. Every single time you open up to imagination you create a more vivid scene to revisit. Like a gym regime, it gets easier the more you exercise this "mind focus" muscle.

When the sea is calm, you can easily see the horizon, and in the same way when your mind is clear, you can "see" your future dreams. In other words, you can envision what you want easily when you are already in your Real Self. This is an important point: "trying to visualise" when you

don't feel good will connect you with the lower self mind's nightmares and worries and misleading fantasies, whereas feeling good first and then relaxing into the vision (envisioning) will connect you with visual ideas of your dream life that you may not have even conceived of. Envisioning isn't wishful thinking or making something up, like daydreaming; it's tuning into the vision of your Real Self.

WHAT TO DO RIGHT NOW

Envisioning

- Lie down or sit comfortably. Close your eyes. Fully relax the body and the mind. This prevents your thoughts and your physical senses arguing with your inner reality and battling your visualisation.

- Declare to yourself the subject of your visualisation. For example this could be a great body, a perfect relationship or a dream career. Now listen within and see what reveals itself to you; wait as the image becomes more vivid in your mind. Come back to the subject of the vision and wait again for a few moments as the images becomes clearer.

- Relax into the images that begin to appear in your mind. Don't try too hard; this exercise is about relaxing into what you see. It's not about forcing or "trying to visualise" - it's about relaxing and letting the images come to you

(Guided audios are available at www.michaeljames.be).

- You may want to choose a vision which is already in an area you have some self-belief. In other words, build on your "baseline": imagine being a successful singer, if you know you can sing well. Or feel yourself winning a huge sporting event, if you're already an athlete with some training behind you. Of course, you don't have to do this, but it makes it easier and more enjoyable if you go into a visualisation on a subject you already have some self-confidence about and moves it beyond ineffective "wishful thinking" or "trying to believe".

- Remember that you are visualising purely for the great feeling of it. You look forward to your envisioning for the simple reason that it feels good. It's less about the content of the images and all about the good feelings. It's about asking "What is it that I need to know?" and then waiting for the answers to come, if they're supposed to, in the moment.

- A good time to envision is while you are in bed, either just before you go to sleep or just after you wake up. In these sleepy states your intellect is less sharp and, therefore, less likely to disagree with this playful practice.

- In order to envision effectively you want to be relaxed and clear-minded. The purpose of this technique is to connect you with the feeling of excitement or passion. If you don't feel good during this exercise, then come out of it and do something else. Envisioning isn't about trying to visualise, but allowing a vision to flash across your mind. It immediately satisfies your longings and gives you what you want, now. If you are not feeling satisfied when you envision, you're missing the point.

- If you use this technique to try to improve or fix a problem situation you have, it won't make you feel good. Don't run before you can walk. You first need to detach by doing a technique from the Feeling Low or Feeling Uninspired levels until you are clear-minded, fulfilled and "problem free" - then you can go into a vision for the fun of it. These earlier levels will help you create a solid foundation through meditation and appreciation techniques so your mind has the space and ability to envision effortlessly and naturally.

- You don't really need any more ideas right now - put the book down and enjoy your life.

CONCLUSION

Why it's a challenge to change your life (and how to make it easier)

We cannot get the benefits from the suggested practices in this book just by thinking about them, or reading about them. Now, let's be honest: techniques like the Focal-point technique aren't always that appealing. Just sitting there and deliberately focusing on a sound seems not only boring, but a waste of time. Practices that get you out of overthinking rarely appeal to the lower level mind because the mind's usual chatter of thoughts doesn't get to take part in the process. Your thoughts are hardly likely to suggest you do something that gets you *out of* thoughts.

Because of this, some people can feel very uncomfortable when they begin to meditate, as the mind goes crazy and doesn't want to loosen up and let go. Instead, it constantly thinks a barrage of thoughts, asking over and over "Are we there yet?!" like a bored child on a long journey.

The mind feeling trapped by meditation may have a tantrum like that same child who is told he or she doesn't even get to go away on a trip at all - because the chattering mind doesn't get to go into the silence. This is understandable, and the initial experience of meditation can indeed be one of extreme boredom as I said. However, if you stay with it and try to breathe your way through it then the detachment between "you" and "the mind" will gradually occur.

You should not actively "try to" detach. Your job is to breathe, to focus on some sound or other object of concentration, and gently get your attention out of the way so the process can work by itself, "airlifting" you out of the mind and into the Real Self in the perfect time.

Interestingly, the times you most need meditation - when your mind is a storm – can actually be the most off-putting time to try. This is because when you are in a lower level mood, your thoughts start loudly telling you meditation won't work, or you haven't got the time to do it. It's like a Formula One driver on the track: the last thing he wants to do is pull over into the pit lane. But this short stop is vital. It's a brief moment for him to sit back from the driving seat and let in his expert team to refuel and rejuvenate his car. If he didn't make the pit stop his vehicle wouldn't make the finish, and might even break down completely. The same is true with a technique like meditation: you have to take time to step back from the thinking mind.

And it's the same with all disciplines - from going to the gym, to learning a musical instrument or beginning a new hobby - it's simply easier not to do it.

I often say in my seminars and workshops that the two problems I most frequently hear from people about meditation are: people say they can't quieten their mind and secondly, they just never get round to doing it as it seems so boring and such a waste of time. So you are not alone in your resistance to giving it a go.

Focal-point technique/meditation

I had tried everything, and the specific type of meditation I talk about in this book - the Focal-point technique - is what did it for me, transforming my life experience. Meditation practices that told me to "observe my thoughts" didn't work. For an overthinker like I was, I would chase every thought I was observing, grab hold of it, and analyse it.

Imagine your thoughts like clouds. They seem very solid and meaningful. Beyond the cloud cover of thoughts is the sun - the Real You. As you focus on a consistent note, whatever it may be, *feel for* the consistent sound. Keep coming back to the sound, *breathe into* the sound to keep anchored in your centre.

By focusing fully on something that doesn't activate your thinking mind, you are lifted beyond your mind, and synced with your Real Self perspective. Don't be "wishy washy" with your focus - do it like you *have* to do it, like something depends on it. Give the point of your focus more authority than your thoughts and hold to it.

For me personally, it took several months before I "got it". In the beginning my mind was like a war zone and amped up ferociously the moment I sat down to this practice. I suggest you do this technique every day until you "get it".

Like cutting a path through rock to find a wellspring, once you have found that cavern of stillness within, you can feel your way there much more easily. It's hard work to dig to find a well, yet once you do, your life transforms, and you have the pathway in place to return to again and again. That is why at the beginning of learning all new skills, it is harder, as you haven't yet "found your groove". Once you have developed your muscles, you can get back there more quickly due to muscle memory. In the same way, there is a "meditation memory", which means that once you have deliberately found the Real Self, you can find it again more easily the next time.

If you are "out and about", you can listen for sounds around as you walk. Keep coming back to the sound, breathe into the sound, to keep you in your centre. Allow the sound to hold your focus, breathe into it as it tunes you back to You again; the You that doesn't think, it just *is*.

Getting started

Morning is the best time, as you are getting ready for your day ahead. The day will be totally different depending on who is running the show - the mind chatter which knows nothing or the all-knowing Real Self. *Who is going to lead you?*

You can begin with the Focal-point technique audio available on my website www.michaeljames.be. Once you are practiced with this technique - and please give yourself time to really feel yourself drop in - you probably won't need my words on the audio to guide you.

The words we speak

The words that we speak are thoughts expressed outwards. So it's a good idea to connect with the Real Self, and then speak. Forget the idea of choosing "positive" words - it's not like that at all. It's about pausing and waiting for the Real You to speak. When we just speak before taking time to get into our Real Self - all that comes out is mind chatter: nonsense, opinion, gossip and analysis that keep us lost in this lower self-mindset. The more you pause from speaking "lower self-mind" thoughts, the more you will be anchored in your calm, connected, confident Real Self perspective. Speaking only words from Real Self guidance clears your mind. Complaining keeps you in overthinking. So only speaking what you want in your life is another way to meditate.

Set yourself a challenge to only speak about things that feel good. Mind chatter in words, like with thoughts, gets you nowhere. Feel for the words that are arising. If they are words which appreciate or speak of what you want, let them come. If not, breathe through them. This takes discipline but it's amazing how this practice will change you.

Get into your project/interest/passion

"When you are inspired by some great purpose, some extraordinary project, all your thoughts break their bonds: Your mind transcends limitations, your consciousness expands in every direction, and you find yourself in a new, great and wonderful world. Dormant forces, faculties and talents become alive, and you discover yourself to be a greater person by far than you ever dreamed yourself to be." Patanjali

A common thing that happens when people get really into some new hobby, is that their problems fall away and they feel great.

I met a woman who was always on the front line of a march about something or other, and often in the press. The thing is she found this purposeful and was surrounded by likeminded people, and it was exciting for her; it "got her in" to her Real Self.

In a similar way, you want to find your own project or interest that's more compelling than your dramas. Someone once told me that good news doesn't sell. I told them that I disagreed, that it's *dull* news that doesn't sell. As amazing as the headline "Thousands of New Trees Planted" may be - it's simply not going to get the attention in the way some catastrophe will. You want to choose an exciting and engaging hobby to pull your attention from your overthinking. *You want to choose a hobby more dynamic than your dramas.*

The follow through

Watching sports on television is a very different experience than becoming a sports champion. Making the decision to change and then following through with the actions required is the vital first step to becoming the star of your own life, rather than an observer or fan of others. Having a discipline, a focus, moving the body; having something to do is vital for syncing you up with your Real Self. It's not so much what you do, but your *commitment* to doing something that changes your life.

When debating whether or not to give the techniques in this book a go, it is not a good idea to listen to that low-level chatter of thoughts running through your mind. This mind chatter feels stressful and will always challenge you to begin tomorrow or in a week's time. Then your mind becomes full of reasons why these exercises won't work, and comes up with suggestions of other, often useless, things to do instead. This lower level chatter of thoughts occurs most strongly in the less than good moods, and can be persuasive. To put it in simple terms: my advice to get over this mind chatter is to ignore that voice and start somewhere. Open this book at random in the Quick Reference Section, and follow the instructions there.

The second wind

At a certain point during a run novices and experienced runners alike talk of a "second wind". This is the point when even though your body feels exhausted suddenly you relax and another burst of energy comes through. However, you need to give the running, or the techniques suggested here, long enough to get to your second wind. Just when you feel like giving up is exactly the time you need to keep on going. Keep up and you will be kept up.

I suggest you make a commitment and give your all to having a go at the techniques. This doesn't mean investing a massive amount of time or effort, and as I've suggested already, trying too hard is counterproductive. But if we return to the gym analogy, we know that doing one push up occasionally will give different results than doing a full workout regularly.

It's also important that you appreciate yourself for what you are doing, even if you have not yet quite managed to throw yourself into the practice wholeheartedly. Remember to remind yourself how well you are doing and how far you have come.

Discouragement

Everyone feels discouraged sometimes. However, if you feel discouraged it is important to continue with your practice regardless, even if you don't feel your changes are consistently happening. You may initially go a few steps forward and a few back. Some days everything may seem hopeless, and that's okay; nothing has gone wrong. It's the same with learning any new skill. Keep on going with your practice, even if you don't feel like it. To prevent your mind wandering into trying to fix the problem, go back to your Appreciation List or mantras.

There is a saying that it is always the darkest before the dawn. Sometimes people tell me that although they are feeling better, their symptoms seem to be getting worse, or things appear to be moving in the wrong direction within a relationship. What they are experiencing is the beginnings of change - which is a good sign. Just keep on going, and keep on doing the exercises.

Developing patience

You don't walk out of the gym on your first visit with your dream body, nor the second, third or even tenth time. But you carry on exercising anyway, trusting and enjoying the process. It may take many months before you achieve the results you want. But in the meantime, you keep on going. Rome wasn't built in a day. Have patience with yourself.

Don't try to "escape" from your feelings too quickly. You don't want to use this book to deny your feelings at all. Sometimes you may want some time in anger or pain or loneliness or whatever. And that's fine. When you are ready to move on to a better feeling, you can. But there is no rush - give yourself permission to experience any feelings you have, reminding yourself it is part of being human.

Don't be ashamed when you feel bad or miss your practice

Some people feel the low emotions more powerfully, but know that nothing has gone wrong. When an Olympic athlete misses their practice, it affects them more than when an amateur misses it. In the beginning, I used to miss my daily practices and then feel almost embarrassed that I "had" to do anything at all, "when most normal people just feel good on their own, without doing these daily lists or meditations", my mind told me. But then I realised I didn't want a normal life - *I wanted an Olympic life*. And it was the same for the above-averagely successful, happy people I met. Their secret was so often a morning ritual to anchor themselves in their Real Self.

Your Real Self constantly shines, and as you go into thoughts, although your light may be covered and seem to dim, your Real Self is expanding and evolving and shines brighter. So no matter what mood you find yourself in, it's all beneficial. You lost your temper and said things you didn't mean? So what! It's all causing your evolution. The best Olympic athletes, if you caught them going through hard training, would hardly seem Olympic calibre, lying there exhausted. And yet it is this training that makes them great. You don't "shame" them for being shaky in training, so why shame someone (or yourself) for going into the "training" of low moods and overthinking? These very moments are the evolution of our greatness. We all have these points of evolution, and it's part of life - and it's to be accepted fully.

Thoughts will come, just as a surfer knows waves will come. The surfer doesn't try to stop the waves - it would be boring if the sea was calm all the time. Instead, the surfer learns how to work with the waves and surf over them. It's the same with us and our thoughts. We want to find a way to navigate through the storms of the overthinking, lower level mind. At times a wave will catch us off guard and we might go under for a while, but like the surfer, we'll come back up all the stronger because of it.

Going under a wave doesn't mean we've failed. It means evolution. When we are in the midst of it, under a wave, it doesn't work to "try to" make this moment great. It's not great right now - but it will pass into greatness.

Self-confidence

Make a decision to dwell on the things you like - and train yourself into this habit. But this task is not always easy. Sometimes your mind will wander on to subjects you don't feel good about, and you'll get temporarily lost in overthinking or you may feel down from time to time. Remember that these moments are valid too; they are the springboard into your evolution, and are all a valuable part of this life's journey. So no matter where you are, or how you feel, everything is okay: everything is just the way it is supposed to be. Remember self-confidence isn't just about loving yourself in the good times - it's about loving yourself in *all* times.

When you have self-confidence, your life works. And without it, even if everything that "should" make you happy is in place, you won't be happy. So liking yourself and feeling good about who you are is vital for living a good life.

The Lighthouse of your Real Self is always shining

The Real Self exists in every moment, waiting for you to tune to it. It is a constant stream of ever evolving confidence. Like a lighthouse it stands, beaming consistently.

You are always doing the best you can and Life is always getting better for you, regardless of how it manifests in any one moment. Use this book to allow yourself to feel okay about wherever you are and relax your way into your self-confidence; your fully expressed Real Self, which is your natural state. *And then live your life.*

MY STORY *About the Author*

"The lamps are different, but the Light is the same"
Rumi

We all have our different stories, of how we wandered off path and then found our way back to our light again, but the essence is the same for all of us. And it's an ongoing journey. Here is my story so far:

At school, I was encouraged to take subjects where I had to *really* think, to "use my mind": Physics, Chemistry and Advanced Mathematics rather than the Arts. The Arts were seen as a "waste of a good mind" and, as I had a great mind, why waste it? It seemed logical, as everyone was saying it.

Society trains us to analyse and to develop our judgments and calls that "intelligence"; something we ought to aspire to. But this approach doesn't work very well - except to get us good at crossword puzzles, perhaps, or sharing our opinion at dinner parties. It is impulse and intuition (your Real Self) that orchestrates everything good on this planet and is the pathway to all that you want. The ideas I've shared with you in this book may seem "unintelligent" to the mind, but they lead you to the true intelligence you are seeking.

I got good grades. And yet I was gradually getting more miserable. My educational mind training just got me to overthink everything, and find solutions to nothing, especially when it came to how to live life. My first major difficulty came up when I began to feel attracted to the same sex, and although to me it felt natural, I slowly discovered it "wasn't ok" in the opinions of pretty much everyone around me. Beginning to dread the effects of being "found out", I spiralled into overthinking and depression, which became the norm for me. Condemnation seemed to come at me from all sides: classmates, teachers, even my GP (who advised me not to mention my feelings again as I wouldn't want it on my medical records as it would "go against me"). I was told I was destined for a life of misery and I didn't feel I fitted in anywhere. My experience with religion was the worst, and I had many detrimental experiences and rejections from its followers who claimed to speak for God.

There was nowhere for me to turn. Little did I know at that point that it was *my thinking* which was steadily building my own jail cell rather than the outside world. The subject matter was irrelevant, the fact was I was creating a battle and the outer world was reflecting that battle. I was at war with Life and felt like a total victim.

Back then, I thought I *was* my overthinking mind, and I was basically at the whim of it. If I felt good and was clear-minded, things went well. But when my mind decided to get really active - which was most of the time - my experience was ruined.

When I moved to college, things got worse. My life became hell. The voices of others - society, teachers, family expectations, the media at large - made me feel I couldn't be myself - and I tormented myself for it. My mind was ferociously self-destructive and my previously A-grades went downhill. I just didn't care anymore.

Feeling I had nowhere left to go, I reached out to drugs. The comedowns which seemed to last days for others seemed to last months for me. I went to the doctors and was prescribed anti-depressants and tranquilizers, but nothing worked. In my personal life, my fearful overthinking led me into an underground world and I started meeting increasingly "dangerous" people and getting involved in risky situations and relationships that ended in pain and heartbreak. I was still living at home with my parents and remember having the thought that I'd never be able to get any kind of job and certainly wouldn't be able to move out and have my independence.

I spent many of the summers of that time alone in my bedroom, curtains drawn, smoking, drinking and listening to angsty music that railed against the world in blame. I was driving myself deeper into victimhood; a self-created prison of overthinking. The sunnier it got outside, the more miserable I felt, as that meant I had to wear less clothing. I never wore T-shirts as I was so insecure about my body, so the weather just added more misery to me. The bright weather also made me think of the fun other people were having whilst I was in hell. My compulsive behaviour became ever more inventive and I got into addictions as a way of trying to cope.

I would have panic attacks in the middle of the poorly paid temporary jobs I occasionally got, and had to leave unannounced, driving to the nearest "Samaritans" (a suicide prevention organisation in the UK) to talk to someone and get a break. This lost me jobs but probably saved my life, as I erred in and out of considering all kinds of things as a way out of it all.

As dramatic as this seems, all along I appeared to much of the world like a pretty normal guy, despite this inner hell. I don't know how I "kept it together" externally as much as I did, and this seems to be the way for many of us: we go it alone, in isolation, our work colleagues and families oblivious to the full extent of the torture chamber going on in our minds.

Self hell to Self-help

With everything building like a pressure cooker, finally I had the "snap" of a nervous breakdown. I went to bed and didn't get up for weeks. My parents were full of worry about me, but in their well-intentioned trying-to-fix-me approach, I only got more lost. Nothing and no one could reach me.

I can't remember exactly the details of when a sliver of light broke through the armour of my thoughts, but there was a day when I pulled myself out of bed and went into the nearby town centre. I stumbled into the "self-help" section of my local bookshop, vision blurred, and grabbed the book nearest to me. Something in me made me walk up to the till and buy this book - even though I remember thinking the title and cover "looked weird". I got home, snuggled under a duvet and began to read... and read some more. I couldn't put it down. A new perception was opening up to me as I read that we somehow have a choice in our focus and our feelings, rather than just letting the mind have its way with us. It seemed we could direct our lives in some way. After using the simple relaxation techniques in the book (which I now realise looking back was my first experience of deliberately dropping into my Real Self) - I began to get moments of peace and started to wake up to being "me" again for the first time since a child. And so started my journey back. But there was still a long way to go.

I landed a dream job in television journalism, working for companies such as ITV and the BBC and travelling the world. My mind was beginning to be less self-punishing. I was becoming more of my Real Self, only I didn't know it at the time.

But this break from the storms was temporary. Yet another broken relationship pushed me back into my familiar vicious cycle. I became trapped in my mind, which became my worst enemy yet again. The thing is, at this point, I didn't see myself as trapped in my mind because I still thought that I *was* this mind. It's like having no knowledge of the sun, and from your position of being in the middle of clouds, you just assume that everything is eternally grey.

I threw myself into the world of self-help, buying book after book. Using the information I read, I found myself trying hard to think positively, to "love myself" to "just be" - only I couldn't do it. I couldn't just "get present" and "stay in the Now" whatever that meant. When I had a problem, the thoughts would surround me like a tornado and I would chase them, grabbing them, taking me down into the darkness again. And my depressions, which had never really left me for long, came in thick and fast with a vengeance.

Another week, another book: the authors talking about how they simply said "I love myself" a few times and were able to feel fantastic - or repeated a couple of happy sounding sentences and found themselves experiencing inner peace. I wondered what was wrong with *my* mind. My mind was nothing like that - it spoke in a loud and frenzied commentary of self-hate, judgment, jealousy, resentment and fear too loud for these positive statements to even register. There was no way I could do the things the books asked of me. I felt ashamed that I "wasn't good enough" to follow these theories. No book or course was enough to deal with *my* cobra-like mind, which was a storm of overthinking, fear and self-hatred.

Thanks to my job in the media (which I had somehow managed to hold down throughout it all), and my own interest in searching for a cure for my debilitating low moods, I managed to meet and interview some huge names in the personal development world. And so I had burning questions for myself to ask these experts, such as "What do you do when you are in the middle of negative overthinking and although you try to be happy, it just takes you down?"

I remember one such interview with a certain woman, who was a very well-known and highly respected speaker: As I asked her what she herself did to deal with overthinking and emotional storms, I noticed her pause and awkwardly shift in her chair. In that moment, I realised that as big as she was in this field, this was a question that blindsided her; I could tell that she hadn't found the answer for this one. Her mood changed, and she hurriedly ended the interview. In my mind's eye I got impressions of her off stage, away from her fans, writhing around in pain and lost in the darkness. If she couldn't do it, what hope was there for a "normal" person like me?

What I learnt from exploring the contemporary personal development world, was that much of the teachings were like school education - about acquiring information and then, you were promised, you would "get there". This was a nice idea - but it wasn't working. I met very few people who had "got there" - including many of the authors themselves.

Some of the interviews I did were very helpful, however. I learned from one teacher I liked, Esther Hicks, that people like me who felt emotions deeply and also had the tendency to overthink would realise, once the mind was mastered, what a huge gift it was. My question, though, was the same: *How* do I do this? *How* do I master the mind and get to the place where what was once a curse becomes an actual *advantage* in living life?

I continued to study, and meet with teachers who were well-respected and considered greats, but I still couldn't find what I was looking for. Maybe the answer was there, but I couldn't see it.

So I was determined to find the answer myself.

The beginning of my research and support groups

Slowly, new ideas formed. I continued my in-depth study of world religions, philosophies and spiritual paths (an interest I had had since my early teens), getting up close and personal with some influential "gurus" along the way, stories of which would make a book in itself. I embarked on a counselling course as I began to get my life together, as I knew my mission was to somehow help others once I'd "got it" for myself. But I was in no rush, as I had little interest in being a teacher like some of the ones I had interviewed: someone with a Wizard of Oz frontage that looked really good but was a wreck "behind closed doors". I wanted to be confident and authentic in my teachings. I realise that we teach who we are more than what we say, and I didn't want to perpetuate a false message - there was enough of that out there, and this was important to me.

After moving to London, and getting involved behind the scenes in personal development organisations, I started a group where I would get together with people and find out what was working and what wasn't. Soon I realised I wasn't the only one tired of being promised that I could "get everything I wanted in seven easy steps" with little or no results. I had thought there was something wrong with me, but then I discovered that there were a lot more people who "weren't getting it" either.

On my journey, some of the first books I read were very complicated, and subsequent books got more and more simple as I "advanced" in my understanding. The truth is simple, so simple a child can "get it" (and often does) - and so simple that adults often ignore it. The Real Self's intuition is simple, the lower self's mind chatter can get very complicated, analytical and always trying to "figure things out".

I remember someone coming to one of my groups in the early days and asking me, "Is this a beginner's group or an advanced group?" I could tell where she was coming from, as she saw herself as really "advanced" in the subject. I explained that both are the same, and I could feel that what I was teaching seemed so simple to her analytical mind that she just couldn't believe it could be the answer she was looking for. Several years later, she returned, and was finally ready to surrender her analytical approach. Sometimes, it seems, people have to go down all the dead ends of thoughts and the pain that it entails before they "get it" and realise their mind's way isn't working. It never has and never will. That was her experience - and mine as well. We "get it" in the perfect time for us.

A system that works

The group became very popular, with the room packed to capacity many weeks of the year. It became a sanctuary for people looking to feel better about themselves and their lives.

Through working with people and listening to their experiences, I noticed themes, and began to develop a system that worked in a very powerful way for people, creating successful workshops and powerful one-to-one sessions. Which brings me to today. Here I stand, clear- minded, empowered and a light to myself and others. The life I have written about is unrecognisable from the life I live today. Are the storms over? No, not entirely, nor would I want them to be as I realise that they are the source of my evolution. But they occur totally different to me nowadays - and I have the tools to deal with them.

AFTERWORD

Lighthouses can be a sad and lonely sight when their light is off, but once they shine, they become attractive and powerful. When you connect with the light of your Real Self, everything will fall into place for you. Community will find you. Your natural charisma will radiate. The fully illuminated lighthouse symbolises that state of *steadfast confidence* where you are feeling whole, complete and fulfilled.

This is the new understanding: an intense way of being is actually a gift. Nothing went wrong and nothing is wrong with any "negativity" you may have gone through - it's all resistance training. The dark times are not "bad" and you will come through them all, stronger, more refreshed and with more talents and skills honed than before. As you reveal who you are, as you move out of needing light from out there because you are *being the light* - you will attract likeminded people to you. Life will mirror back your greatness precisely because you don't need it, you *are* it.

Don't force anything with these ideas - it's a gentle dropping into who you are; a relaxing into this pool of confidence that is the Real Self; an instant connecting with the knowing that All is well; a going with the flow. When we find a way to relax, we are pulled in and synced up with ourselves.

Allow yourself to be tuned into the clarity and confidence of who you are. And then be the lighthouse that you were born to be. This is the best thing you can do for yourself, your loved ones, and the entire planet. We want to connect and shine bright not just for ourselves - but because we never know who is looking to *our* light to guide them home.

Michael

For further resources and to find out more about Michael's seminars, workshops and one-to-one appointments visit **www.michaeljames.be**